FAVOURITE FARMHOUSE RECIPES

compil[ed by]
Carole Gregory

with illustrations
by A. R. Quinton

SALMON

INDEX

Cover pictures: *front* Priory Cottages, Steventon, Oxfordshire
back Cottage at Elmley Castle, Worcestershire

Printed and Published by J. Salmon Ltd., Sevenoaks, England ©

Farmhouse Chicken Casserole

4 large chicken joints
1 clove garlic, crushed
1½ lb. scraped small new potatoes
4 rashers streaky bacon, de-rinded and diced
4 sticks celery, washed and sliced
12 baby onions, peeled
4 oz. button mushrooms
2 oz. butter
Salt and black pepper
1 pint chicken stock
1 heaped teaspoon mixed herbs
1 bayleaf
1 teaspoon paprika
1 oz. seasoned flour
Chopped parsley for garnish

Set oven to 350°F or Mark 4. Toss the chicken joints in seasoned flour. Melt the butter in a frying pan and brown the joints in the butter until golden all over. Place the joints in a large casserole dish and add the potatoes. Place the garlic, onions, bacon, celery and mushrooms in the pan and cook for a few minutes. Add remainder of the flour and stir in well. Add the stock gradually, stirring constantly. Add the herbs and paprika and check the seasoning. Pour over the chicken and potatoes. Add the bayleaf. Cover and cook for about 1–1¼ hours until tender. Remove the bayleaf and garnish with parsley. Serve with carrots. Serves 4.

The Village – Wyre Piddle, Worcestershire

Egg, Bacon and Leek Pie

6 oz. shortcrust pastry
4 oz. leeks, washed and very thinly sliced
6 oz. streaky bacon, diced
4 eggs
Salt and black pepper
Pinch of freshly grated nutmeg

Set oven to 400°F or Mark 6. Line a 7 inch round pie dish with pastry. Place the thinly sliced leeks on the pastry, then the layer of bacon and lastly break the 4 eggs on top. Season, add the nutmeg and cover with a thin layer of pastry. Bake for about 40 minutes. Serve hot with a green vegetable or cold with chutney and salad. Serves 4.

Belly Pork with Red Cabbage

1 medium red cabbage, finely shredded
2 oz. bacon dripping
1 lb. de-rinded belly pork, cut into cubes
1 large cooking apple, peeled and diced
1 small onion, finely chopped
4 oz. lean bacon, diced
Rind and juice of 1 orange
3 level tablespoons sugar
3 level tablespoons wine vinegar
Pinch of mixed dried herbs
$1/4$ pint chicken stock
Pinch of freshly ground nutmeg and pepper

Set oven to 300°F or Mark 2. In a large pan melt the dripping and add the bacon, pork, onion and apple. Stir for a few minutes and sprinkle with herbs. Mix the stock, sugar and vinegar together. Meanwhile wash the cabbage well in salted water. Place the shredded cabbage in the pan and mix all the ingredients well. Add the liquid and place in a large buttered casserole. Cover and bake for about 2 hours. Serves 4. Nice with baked potatoes and a cold meat selection.

COUNTRY CHICKEN

4 large chicken joints
6 medium sized potatoes, cubed
1/2 head celery, chopped
Salt
Freshly ground black pepper
1/4 lb. sliced mushrooms
Pinch freshly ground nutmeg
Bayleaf
1/2 pint chicken stock
2 oz. butter
2 onions, thinly sliced
1 tablespoon chopped parsley
4 oz. packet frozen peas

Set oven to 350°F or Mark 4. Skin the chicken joints and fry them in the butter until golden brown. Place in a warmed casserole dish. Then fry the onions and add to the pan all the other ingredients except the peas. When heated through pour over the chicken. Cover and cook for 30 minutes. Add the peas and cook for a further 15 minutes. Serves 4.

TURKEY PIE

1 lb. cooked, diced turkey
1 small onion, chopped
2 oz. butter
1 tablespoon sherry
1 tablespoon chopped parsley
or chives
1½ lb. mashed potato beaten
with 1 small egg
15 oz. can condensed soup
of your choice
¼ lb. packet sweetcorn
Black pepper

Set oven to 325°F or Mark 3. Fry the onion in butter for a few minutes. Stir in the diced turkey, sweetcorn and herbs; season with pepper. Gradually stir in the soup and sherry and continue stirring until heated. Place in an ovenproof dish. Top with the mashed potato. Bake for 30–40 minutes and serve with a green vegetable and chutney. Serves 4.

The Village Smithy – Penshurst, Kent

Picnic Pasty

12 oz. shortcrust pastry
1 large onion, peeled and finely chopped
1 large potato, peeled and diced
1 large carrot, peeled and diced
4 oz. runner beans or celery, chopped
8 oz. cold cooked meat or corned beef
Seasoning to taste
2 tablespoons gravy or stock
Pinch of mixed herbs

Set oven to 400°F or Mark 6. Place the onion, potato, carrot and beans or celery in a saucepan. Cover with boiling water and cook for 5 minutes. Meanwhile line a rectangular 10 x 12 inch shallow tin with half the pastry. Drain the vegetables, add the seasoning, herbs, cooked meat or corned beef, gravy or stock and mix well. Cover the pastry with filling to within 1 inch of the top. Brush edges with water and cover with another layer of pastry. Seal the edges. Brush the top with milk and bake for 40 minutes until golden. Eat hot or cold. Serve with chutney and salad.

SMOKED HADDOCK FLAN

6 oz. shortcrust pastry
1½ lb. smoked haddock, cooked and flaked
2 hard boiled eggs, sliced
1 small onion, thinly sliced
1½–2 lb. cooked creamed potato
2 oz. grated Cheddar cheese
½ pint milk (infused with slice of onion, herbs, bayleaf and peppercorns)
¾ oz. butter
1 rounded tablespoon flour
Salt and pepper

Set oven to 400°F or Mark 6. Place an 8 inch flan ring on a lightly greased baking sheet and line with the pastry. Place the flaked fish on the pastry with the onion on top and sliced eggs around the edge. Melt the butter in a pan, stir in the flour and blend in the strained milk. Add the cheese and season. Stir constantly until it thickens. Spoon the sauce over the flan. Put the creamed potato in a piping bag fitted with a large rose nozzle. Pipe potato around the edge of the flan and across the centre, in a lattice pattern. Place in the oven for 20–30 minutes until brown. Serves 4–5.

The Village Green – Ockley, Surrey

Kidney and Sausage Casserole

6 lamb's kidneys
12 baby onions
1/4 lb. button mushrooms
1 oz. butter
1 oz. flour
1 tablespoon tomato purée
1/2 pint brown stock
1/2 lb. cocktail sausages
1/4 lb. frozen peas
2 tablespoons dry sherry
Salt and pepper

Set oven to 325°F or Mark 3. Heat the fat in a frying pan and cook the onions and mushrooms for 5 minutes, then place in an ovenproof dish. Skin the kidneys, cut them in half and remove the core. Dredge them in the flour and sauté gently for a few minutes. Add the tomato purée, stock and sherry and mix well; pour into the casserole. Cover and bake for about 20 minutes, then add the peas and bake for a further 25 minutes until the kidneys are tender. Meanwhile grill or sauté the sausages until they are golden brown and add to the dish, either whole or cut in half. Serve with potatoes and a vegetable. Serves 6.

Ham and Cheese Toasties

4 slices bread
4 thin slices cooked ham
4 oz. grated cheese
1 tablespoon of your
favourite chutney
1 small beaten egg
Black pepper
Paprika to decorate
4 halved, grilled tomatoes
and watercress to garnish

Toast the bread on one side only. Butter the untoasted side and place a slice of ham on each round of bread. Spread a layer of your favourite chutney over the ham. Mix the cheese, egg and pepper together and spread evenly over the chutney. Place under a hot grill until the cheese melts and is golden brown. Sprinkle paprika over the top and garnish with two halved, grilled tomatoes and a sprig of watercress to each plate. Nice served with Worcestershire Sauce. Serves 4.

GLOUCESTERSHIRE PIE

1 lb. lean lamb, cooked and sliced
1 lb. onions, thinly sliced
1 lb. cooking apples, thinly sliced
2 oz. butter
Pinch of rosemary and nutmeg
$1/2$ pint rich gravy
$1/2$–$3/4$ lb. potatoes, diced
$1/2$–$3/4$ lb. swede, diced
Salt and pepper

Set oven to 375°F or Mark 5. Put the onions and apples in a pan and cover with water. Boil for 5 minutes. Drain well. Meanwhile boil the swede for 10 minutes, then add the potato and cook until both are soft. Drain well and mash together until smooth. Grease an ovenproof dish with the butter. Place layers of meat, onion and apple in the dish, seasoning and sprinkling each layer with herbs as you fill up the dish. Pour in the gravy and top with the mashed potato and swede mixture. Dot the top with butter and bake, uncovered, for $3/4$–1 hour. Serve with a green vegetable. Serves 4.

Cheesey Leeks with Ham

8 leeks
8 thin slices cooked ham
1½ oz. butter
½ oz. flour
½ pint milk
¼ pint water, reserved from cooking leeks
6 oz. grated Cheddar cheese
1 teaspoon made mustard
Salt and black pepper

Wash the leeks well. Cook in salted boiling water until tender; drain well (keeping ¼ pint water for sauce). Wrap a slice of ham around each leek and place in a hot, shallow, buttered ovenproof dish; keep warm. Melt the butter in a pan, add the flour and cook for 1 minute. Remove from the heat and gradually stir in the milk and leek stock. Return to the heat and stir constantly until the mixture thickens. Stir in 4 oz. cheese and the mustard and seasoning. Pour the sauce over the leeks. Sprinkle with the remaining cheese and place the dish under a hot grill until it is brown and bubbling. Serve with wholemeal bread. Serves 4.

The Village Cross – Ripple, Gloucestershire

Minced Beef Casserole

2 lb. lean minced beef
3 tablespoons cooking oil
2 oz. mushrooms, sliced
4 carrots, cubed
1 small can tomatoes
2 sticks celery, sliced
2 large onions, sliced
2 pints water and
2 stock cubes
Pinch of mixed herbs
Salt and pepper
2 teaspoons brown sugar
4 oz. swede or turnip, cubed
3 tablespoons flour

Set oven to 300°F or Mark 2. This dish is best made the day before it is required, to improve the flavour. Heat the oil in large frying pan. Mix the meat with the flour and seasoning and brown well in a pan. Remove to a deep casserole. Put the vegetables in a frying pan and sweat for a few minutes; then add the rest of the ingredients and mix well. Check the seasoning. Pour over the meat and stir well. Cover tightly and cook slowly for about 1½ hours. Serve with French fried potatoes and a green vegetable. Serves 6–8.

Sausage Pie

8 oz. shortcrust pastry
3/4 lb. pork sausage meat
1 small onion, finely chopped
1 level teaspoon chopped chives
1 level teaspoon chopped parsley
2 tablespoons chicken stock
1 small beaten egg
Salt and black pepper

Set oven to 375°F or Mark 5. Line an 8 inch ovenproof pie dish with the pastry. Using only half the quantity of beaten egg, mix all the ingredients together very well, with a fork. Place in a pie dish and level off. Top with a pastry lid; trim and flute the edges with the back of a knife. Glaze a pastry with the remaining beaten egg. Bake for 15 minutes then lower oven temperature to 325°F or Mark 3 for 30–45 minutes until the pie is cooked through. Serve hot with vegetables or cold with salad. Very useful for picnics. Serves 4–6.

ROTTINGDEAN Nᴿ BRIGHTON

A.R.Q.

The Village Pond – Rottingdean, Sussex

CHICKEN AND APPLE CHEESEBAKE

12 oz. cooked chicken
4 oz. butter
4 tablespoons toasted white breadcrumbs
1/2 pint white sauce
4 oz. grated Cheddar cheese
5 Cox's Orange Pippins
Salt and black pepper

Set oven to 400°F or Mark 6. Butter a shallow ovenproof dish. Peel, core and slice 4 of the apples and fry them gently in the butter. Place the chicken in the bottom of the dish and put the apple slices on top. Mix 3 oz. of cheese into the white sauce and pour over the apples. Season. Mix the breadcrumbs with the remaining 1 oz. of cheese and sprinkle over the sauce. Cut the remaining apple into rings (unpeeled) and toss in the butter; arrange neatly on top of the dish. Bake for 20–30 minutes until crisp and golden. Serves 4.

COCK-A-LEEKIE

12 prunes soaked overnight (optional)
1 lb. leeks, trimmed and sliced
one 2½ lb. oven-ready fresh chicken
2 pints water
2 stock cubes
Bouquet garni
Salt and freshly ground black pepper
Cornflour to thicken (if necessary)
Chopped parsley to garnish

Dissolve the stock cubes in the water and add to a large pan with the bouquet garni, chicken and leeks. Bring to the boil and remove any scum. Simmer very gently for 1–1½ hours until the chicken is tender. Remove the chicken from the pan, skin it and cut the meat into neat portions. Return to the pan. Add salt to taste. If using prunes, add now and simmer for 20 minutes. Thicken with a little cornflour mixed to a cream with water and add the chopped parsley. The flavour improves if this dish is made the night before it is required. Serves 4.

Mushroom Soup

2 oz. butter
2 oz. flour
1/2 lb. large mushrooms
2 onions, very finely chopped
2 pints strong chicken stock
1 tablespoon rice
1 bayleaf
Chopped lemon balm to decorate
1 tablespoon dry sherry

Wipe the mushrooms with a damp cloth. Do not peel, but chop them very finely. Melt 1 oz. butter, add the onion and mushrooms and cook for a few minutes, covered. Remove the lid, add the rest of the butter; when melted stir in the flour and the stock. Add the rice, bayleaf and seasoning. Simmer very gently for 20 minutes until the rice is tender. Remove the bayleaf and check the seasoning. Add the sherry. Garnish with lemon balm or a herb of your choice. Serves 4–6.

Turkey Broth

2 oz. butter
1 onion, finely chopped
1 large carrot, finely cubed
8 oz. potato, cubed
1 stick celery, chopped
8 oz. cooked turkey, diced
4 oz. peas
4 oz. runner beans, sliced
1 oz. flour
Pinch of mixed herbs
1 teaspoon curry powder
1½ pints turkey or game stock
½ pint creamy milk
Salt and pepper
Parsley
Pinch of paprika to garnish

Melt the butter in a pan and add all the vegetables except the peas and beans. Stir in the curry powder and cook for a few minutes. Add the flour and gradually stir in the stock. Add the herbs and simmer gently for 40 minutes. Add the peas, beans and turkey meat and simmer for 15 minutes, then add the milk and parsley. When hot, serve into bowls and sprinkle paprika on top of each bowl. Serves 6.

The Village Inn – Waltham St. Laurence, Berkshire

Summer Soup

1 onion, finely chopped
1 rasher of bacon, cubed
2 large heads of lettuce, cleaned and shredded
2 oz. butter
2 oz. flour
1/2 cucumber, peeled and cubed
Salt and pepper
1 potato, cubed
3/4 pint chicken or ham stock
3/4 pint milk
Pinch of mixed herbs
Croutons to garnish

Melt the butter in a large pan. Slowly sauté the onion, bacon, cucumber and potato. Mix well. Add the lettuce, cover and cook for 5 minutes. Sprinkle in the flour and seasoning and mix. Add the herbs and stock. When it thickens add the milk and simmer gently until the potato is cooked. Put in a blender for a few minutes. Return to the pan, heat through and serve with fried croutons. Serves 4–6.

Lemon Dessert

1 packet trifle sponges or
1 home-made fatless
sponge
4 oz. soft margarine
4 oz. caster sugar
4 eggs, separated
2 large lemons
1/4 pint double cream
5 glacé cherries
5 chocolate squares

Well butter a 1 lb. loaf tin. Cream the margarine and sugar until fluffy. Add the egg yolks. Whisk the egg whites until stiff and fold into the mixture then add the grated rind and juice of the 2 lemons. Do not worry if it curdles. Cut the sponges lengthways and put a layer of sponge on the base of the tin then a layer of lemon mixture, alternately, finishing with a layer of sponge on top. Cover with foil and place in the refrigerator for 24 hours. Turn out on to a flat, rectangular or oval dish. Completely cover with whipped cream and decorate the top with a line of cherries and chocolate squares placed alternately. Serve chilled. Serves 5–6.

MARTYRS WORTHY
Nr WINCHESTER

A.R.QUINTON

The Water Meadows – Martyrs Worthy, Hampshire

SUMMER PUDDING

5 oz. whipped cream
1–1½ lb. fruit (a mixture of raspberries, strawberries, blackberries, blackcurrants)
Sugar to taste
Scant ¼ pint water
4–6 slices medium sliced bread, crustless

Take a 2 pint pudding basin, or souflée dish. Cut the bread to fit the base and sides of the dish. Put the blackberries and blackcurrants and sugar to taste into a pan with the water. Simmer gently until almost soft, add the raspberries and strawberries and cook for a further 3 minutes. Put the mixture in the basin (reserving 2–3 ozs. juice). Top with the bread, pressing down firmly. Cover the basin with a plate or saucer to fit the top exactly. Place a weight on top and leave in the refrigerator overnight. Turn out on to a serving dish just before serving. Use the reserved juice to cover any parts of the bread which have been left white. Serve with whipped cream. Serves 4–6.

Raspberry Cake

4 oz. soft margarine
4 oz. caster sugar
2 beaten eggs
5 oz. self-raising flour
1 packet raspberry flavoured cornflour
1 tablespoon warm water
1/2 lb. fresh raspberries
5 oz. whipped cream

Set oven to 375°F or Mark 5. Grease and line two 7 inch cake tins. Cream the margarine and sugar until fluffy then add the eggs, sifted flour and cornflour; lastly add the water. Mix well. Halve the mixture, put it into the tins and bake for about 20 minutes until firm. Sandwich with whipped cream and raspberries sweetened to taste.

Brown Bread Ice Cream

¹/₂ pint double cream
¹/₄ pint single cream
2 eggs, separated
1 tablespoon rum
4 oz. brown breadcrumbs
3 oz. sifted icing sugar

Whisk the double cream until stiff and then gradually whisk in the single cream. Fold in the sugar and breadcrumbs. Whisk together the egg yolks and rum. Fold into the mixture. Lastly, stiffly beat the egg whites and fold in. Freeze for at least 4 hours before serving. Serves 6.

GOOSEBERRY FLAN

2 heads of elderflower
1 lb. gooseberries, topped and tailed
6 tablespoons white wine
2 beaten eggs
$1/4$ pint double cream
4 tablespoons clear honey, warmed
Pinch of salt
Pinch of nutmeg
An 8 inch flan ring lined with shortcrust pastry

Set oven to 375°F or Mark 5. Place the fruit in a saucepan with the elderflower and wine. Cover and simmer very gently until the fruit is tender. This takes about 20 minutes. Remove the elderflowers. Stir the mixture and beat well with a fork then rub through a sieve into a clean bowl. Add the warmed honey then the beaten eggs, nutmeg, salt and cream. Mix well and pour into the pastry case. Bake for about 40 minutes until firm and golden brown. Leave on a wire tray to cool. Serve chilled with a jug of cream. Serves 6.

The Village Church – Shere, Surrey

GINGER GRIDDLE SCONES

8 oz. flour
2 oz. margarine
2 oz. caster sugar
Pinch of salt
¼ pint of milk
1 level teaspoon bicarbonate
of soda
2 level teaspoons cream
of tartar
1 level teaspoon ground
ginger

Sift the flour, salt, bicarbonate and ginger into a bowl. Rub in the fat and stir in the sugar. Dissolve the cream of tartar in the milk and bind the mixture to form a soft dough. Knead and divide into two portions. Form each portion into a circle and cut into four. Place the 8 scones on a hot griddle and cook for 5 minutes on each side. Serve warm.

DATE AND WALNUT CAKE

8 oz. chopped dates
1 teaspoon bicarbonate of
soda
3 oz. butter
8 oz. sugar
1 large egg
1 teaspoon vanilla essence
10 oz. flour
1 teaspoon baking powder
$1/2$ teaspoon salt

Icing
$2^{1}/_{2}$ tablespoons demerara
sugar
1 tablespoon butter
1 tablespoon cream
Chopped walnuts for
decoration

Pour one breakfast cup of boiling water over 8 oz. chopped dates and add 1 teaspoon bicarbonate of soda. Let this stand while mixing the main ingredients. Grease and line a 12 inch x 9 inch cake tin. Set oven to 350°F or Mark 4. Cream the butter and sugar. Add the beaten egg. Stir in the vanilla essence. Add the flour, baking powder and salt. Add the date mixture to the cake mixture and mix well. Put into the tin and bake for 40 minutes. Cover with icing.

Icing – Mix the ingredients in a large pan. Bring to the boil for 3 minutes stirring constantly. Allow to cool a little and pour over the cake. Scatter with chopped walnuts.

THE OLD MILL DUNSTER

A.R.QUINTON

The Watermill – Dunster, Somerset

Sultana Cake

1 lb. sultanas
8 oz. butter
12 oz. caster sugar
1 level teaspoon mixed spice
1 tablespoon marmalade
2 level teaspoons baking powder
Pinch of salt
3 beaten eggs
12 oz. flour

Grease and line a round 10 inch tin. Set oven to 325°F or Mark 3. Put the fruit in a large saucepan – barely cover with cold water. Bring to the boil and boil for 5 minutes. Drain the fruit well. Add the butter, cut up in small pieces, to the fruit in the pan. Stir until it has melted and add the marmalade. Leave to cool while you sift the flour, salt and spice into a large bowl. Beat the sugar and eggs together well, add to the flour mixture and lastly add the fruit mixture. Blend well. Pour into the prepared tin. Bake for 1 hour then lower the temperature to 300°F or Mark 2 and bake for a further 30 minutes. Cool on a wire rack. This cake improves in flavour if left for 48 hours before cutting.

SHORTBREAD BISCUITS

6 oz. butter
2 oz. icing sugar
8 oz. self-raising flour

Grease baking trays. Set oven to 350°F or Mark 4. Cream the butter and icing sugar together until very soft and fluffy. Gradually add the sifted flour and knead lightly. On a lightly floured surface, roll out to $1/8$–$1/4$ inch thickness. Cut with a plain or fluted cutter. Place on trays and bake for 8–10 minutes until pale brown. Cool on a wire rack. Nice served with a sprinkling of sifted icing sugar on top at coffee time, or to accompany fruit desserts.

Buttermilk Cake

12 oz. currants
4 oz. sultanas
2 oz. glacé cherries
1 lb. flour
3 beaten eggs
4 oz. butter
4 oz. margarine
8 oz. demerara sugar
2 level teaspoons baking powder
2 level teaspoons bicarbonate of soda
1 level teaspoon cream of tartar
¼ level teaspoon salt
¼ level teaspoon ground ginger
1 level teaspoon grated nutmeg
½ pint buttermilk (or use 1 tablespoon vinegar made up to ½ pint with fresh milk)

Set oven to 325°F or Mark 3. Grease and line a square 9 inch cake tin. Cream together the butter, margarine and sugar. Add the eggs, the sifted dry ingredients and the buttermilk. Stir in the fruit. Mix well. Turn into the tin and bake for 1½–2 hours in the centre of the oven until firm. Cool on a wire rack.

Fruit Gingerbread

1 lb. flour
3 oz. sultanas
4 oz. milk
6 oz. butter or margarine
6 oz. treacle
1 rounded teaspoon
bicarbonate of soda
Pinch of salt
2 eggs
4 oz. caster sugar
1 teaspoon ground ginger
6 oz. syrup

Icing
8 oz. icing sugar
1 tablespoon water
1 tablespoon warmed syrup
Crystallised ginger

Set oven to 350°F or Mark 4. Grease and line a square 7 inch tin. Melt the butter, treacle, syrup and sugar together gently in a pan. Sift together the flour, ginger and bicarbonate of soda into a bowl. Add the salt and fruit. Beat the eggs in a separate bowl and add the milk, then add to the flour mixture. To this add the warmed treacle mixture and mix well. Pour into the tin and bake for 45–60 minutes until firm. Cool on a wire rack. May be eaten plain or iced.

Icing – Add the warmed syrup to the sifted icing sugar. If too thick add warmed water carefully until a dropping consistency is achieved. Decorate with crystallised ginger.

The Village Ford – Kersey, Suffolk

OAT SQUARES

8 oz. self-raising flour
8 oz. porridge oats
Pinch of salt
2 level teaspoons ground
ginger
8 oz. hard margarine
2 dessertspoons syrup
6 oz. sugar

Set oven to 325°F or Mark 3. Grease a shallow 14 inch x 9 inch tin. Melt the margarine and syrup in a pan, gently, and add to the remaining ingredients. Mix well. Put into the tin and press down firmly with a fork. Bake for 20–30 minutes until golden brown. Cut into squares whilst warm and leave in the tin until cold. Can be served plain or drizzle the top with melted plain chocolate.

GINGERBREAD MEN

4 oz. butter
8 oz. self-raising flour
4 oz. soft brown sugar
2 teaspoons ground ginger
1 level teaspoon mixed spice
1 tablespoon black treacle
1 tablespoon syrup
1 teaspoon orange juice

Set oven to 350°F or Mark 4. Grease and flour baking trays. Cream together the butter, sugar, treacle, syrup and orange juice. Add the dry ingredients. Knead well. Roll out on to a lightly floured surface. Make a cardboard gingerbread man (or use a shaped cutter) and use as a template to cut out shapes. Place on the baking trays. Bake for 10–15 minutes. Cool for a few minutes before removing from the trays. Decorate with icing.

The Common – Upper Sheringham, Norfolk

DAMSON CHUTNEY

3 lb. cleaned damsons
2 pints malt vinegar
1½ lb. Bramley apples, peeled,
cored and finely diced
1 lb. onions, peeled and
finely chopped
2 teaspoons ground ginger
3 level teaspoons salt
1 lb. soft brown sugar
1 oz. pickling spice
(tied in muslin bag to
handle of pan)

Simmer the damsons in preserving pan with 1 pint vinegar until the fruit is soft enough to remove the stones. When all the stones have been removed, add the apples, onions, ginger, salt and the spice bag, which is tied to pan handle for easy removal later. Cook until the mixture is soft then add the rest of the vinegar and sugar. Stir well until the sugar has dissolved. When the mixture is thick, remove from the heat. Put into warm, clean jars and seal. Leave to mature for 2 months. Nice served with mature cheese and crusty bread. Makes about 7 lb. chutney.

BLACKBERRY CORDIAL

5 lb. cleaned blackberries
2 oz. citric acid
2 pints cold water
Preserving sugar

Place the fruit, water and citric acid in a large bowl. Stir and leave overnight, covered. Next day, strain the juice and to each pint of juice add $1\frac{1}{2}$ lbs. preserving sugar. Bring to the boil and boil for 10 minutes. Leave to cool, then strain through a fine sieve into clean bottles with screw tops.

ELDERFLOWER CHAMPAGNE

4 large heads of elderflower (picked on a sunny July day)
6 pints cold water
2 pints boiling water
1½ lb. granulated sugar
Juice and rind of 2 large lemons
2 tablespoons white wine vinegar

Do not wash the flowers, but remove any insects and the thick stalks. Place the sugar in a very large bowl and cover with 2 pints of boiling water. Stir until the sugar has dissolved. Then add 6 pints cold water, the rind and juice of the lemons, the vinegar and flowers. Stir well. Cover and leave, covered, for 48 hours, stirring occasionally. Strain through a fine sieve into clean bottles with screw tops. Leave an inch gap at the top of each bottle and screw down well. Leave in a cool place to mature. Nice served with ice. Ready to drink in 6 weeks but it tastes better the longer it is left.

METRIC CONVERSIONS

The weights, measures and oven temperatures used in the preceding recipes can be easily converted to their metric equivalents.

Weights

Avoirdupois	Metric
1 oz.	just under 30 grams
4 oz. (¼ lb.)	app. 115 grams
8 oz. (½ lb.)	app. 230 grams
1 lb.	454 grams

Liquid Measures

Imperial	Metric
1 tablespoon (liquid only)	20 millilitres
1 fl. oz.	app. 30 millilitres
1 gill (¼ pt.)	app. 145 millilitres
½ pt.	app. 285 millilitres
1 pt.	app. 570 millilitres
1 qt.	app. 1.140 litres

Oven Temperatures

	°Fahrenheit	Gas Mark	°Celsius
Slow	300	2	140
	325	3	158
Moderate	350	4	177
	375	5	190
	400	6	204
Hot	425	7	214
	450	8	232
	500	9	260

Flour as specified in these recipes refers to Plain Flour unless otherwise described